www.ingramcontent.com/pod-product-compliance
Lightning Source LLC
Chambersburg PA
CBHW071440040426
42445CB00012BA/1404

7 Weeks

to a

Better Marriage

A SEVEN-WEEK STUDY COURSE

BY JIM COTÉ

7 Weeks to a Better Marriage

Copyright © 2014, Jim Coté

ISBN 9780615963334

Printed in the United States

First Edition

1 2 3 4 5 6 7 8 9 10

Cover design: Matt Coté

Editing/inside book design:
Susan K. Elliott, The Write Word

Please visit the website for other great titles
by Jim Coté and Washbasin Publications
www.mastersmen.com

TABLE OF CONTENTS

INTRODUCTION

Marriage — both a boom and a bane depending on whom you talk to. Marriage is a booming business for wedding planners and vendors who provide all the necessary trimmings to the wedding day. It is also a booming business for the lawyers who help couples out of the original covenant they committed to on that wedding day!

It's a bane to married couples going through struggles that seem intractable. And it's a bane to the friends, family members, counselors and others who endure watching couples struggle to regain the joy, enthusiasm, confidence and the romantic spark that originally brought them together.

Believe it or not, marriage is meant by God to be a blessing. If so, we must ask ourselves, how do we get there; how do we achieve what He intends?

Simple. It all comes down to commitment. Now I didn't say simple to do, just simple as a principle of success. As with any success, more often than not it comes down to perspiration more than information or inspiration. So it is with marriage. There is lots of information on the topic – both professional and from friends. There is often much inspiration, especially when you find that you have "fallen in love." But perspiration is the most important ingredient for this issue and perspiration is just a synonym for commitment. Commitment is the first principle of any solid union, marriage especially. This is the primary missing ingredient in marriages today.

How so? First, too many couples don't enter into this sacred union. They are afraid. They lack faith in a God that can do the impossible. It takes faith to believe that God can and will make two distinctly different people better off together than apart. It takes a lifetime of confronting and overcoming challenges to yield the fruit of a marriage that is an enduring blessing. This blessing benefits the couple and the rest of their family, both their children and extended relatives. Today's myopic viewpoint on marriage, where couples decide to live together until "disagreement do us part" instead of entering into a more enduring covenant, shortchanges God's best intent for the male/ female bond.

Second, once married, too many couples view marriage as an endurance race. "How much can I put up with, and can I make it to the end of my life with this person?" they ask, instead of viewing marriage as a long-term investment: "How much can I make this relationship grow and yield before life is over?" Emotionally exhausted couples quit their covenant when they believe its challenges exceed its potential rewards. In other words, they lose sight of a supernatural God who allows life troubles to test their faith and temper the "metal" of their union.

As a result, many couples, left to a human, natural perspective, believe it makes sense to dissolve the union and start over rather than rely on a miraculous God to do something supernatural. Forgetting God's promises to extend His favor in blessing them, they walk away from a chance to see God work wonders in healing their pain, resolving their problems and providing His reward for their perseverance in the covenant they vowed to uphold.

Yes, God has a great and grand design for men and women to follow who have fallen in love. This design underscores His reality, goodness, greatness and the eternal promise that marriage represents.

Let's look at that design now broken down into seven simple commitments as presented in the Bible. Here they are.

1. **Pursuit – Proverbs 18:22**

   a. Best practice for finding the wife of your dreams is to seek the best candidate, intentionally, courageously, honorably and prudently.

   b. If a woman is pursuing you, I'd take some time to consider her motives. Best candidates are sought, not seductive.

2. **Value – Proverbs 18:22**

    a. Scripture is clear, women are to be seen as a good thing, to be cherished, appreciated. Therefore, you should hold that viewpoint from the beginning to end.

    b. We achieve what we believe so believing the best of your wife will move you to treat her best. Treating a woman as a blessing will yield that reality in your relationship. It begins with viewpoint and ends with realization of blessing!

3. **Favor – Proverbs 18:22**

    a. Men often fail to realize that God intends to supernaturally bless them through their wife.

    b. This just underscores two realities: marriage is a spiritually sanctioned union to be held in respect as sacred. Marriage results reflect the wonders of God. All men are better off by being in union with a good woman than without. Many men belittle and berate their wives instead of blessing them ("speak well of"). As a result, men forfeit God's intended blessings. Better to believe God's goodness, nurture your wife and receive His blessings than to miss them through ignorance, stubbornness or neglect.

4. **Conflict – Genesis 3:17**

    a. Sin started a conflict snowball – between man and God and with humans toward one another. In marriage that often looks like two individuals vying for control. God has ordained there be only one lonely spot at the top of the responsibility pyramid – head of the household (1 Corinthians 11).

    b. Man is often relationally lazy. Therefore, he often doesn't lead so women take over, or try to!

5. **Sacrifice – Ephesians 5:25**

    a. Sacrifice is spelled "love" — Christ-like love, *agape*, seeking the best for the object of your love

    b. The return on the investment of *agape* love is a reward that makes it all worthwhile. You get her back "sanctified," in a better position than before, a "best wife"!

6. **Understanding – 1 Peter 3:7**

    a. Be a student of your wife to identify your different strengths

    b. Organize your lives around those strengths, honoring hers and stewarding your own; this is headship responsibility. This is marital leadership!

7. **Respect – Ephesians 5:33**

    a. You can't demand it but you can command it – that is, expect the best and lead her to that conclusion about you.

    b. If you love as Christ loves, you will get the respect you deserve

Pursuit

As described in the introduction, marriage is "both a boom and a bane depending on whom you talk to. Marriage is a booming business for wedding planners and vendors who provide all the necessary trimmings to the wedding day. It is also a booming business for the lawyers who help couples out of the original covenant they committed to on that wedding day!

"It's a bane to the married couples who go through struggles that seem intractable. And it's a bane to the friends, family members, counselors and others who endure watching couples struggle to regain the joy, enthusiasm, confidence and the romantic spark that originally brought them together.

"Believe it or not, marriage is meant by God to be a blessing. If so, we must ask ourselves, how do we get there, how do we achieve what He intends?"

As I emphasized, it all comes down to commitment and that is true. This commitment falls into seven significant parts and the first should indeed be first as everything begins with how we start.

Let's look at how to start this move toward a better marriage by looking at how God intends for us to get there in the first place, by pursuing a wife!

Commentary:

#1 Pursuit - Proverbs 18:22 — "He who finds a wife finds a good thing And obtains favor from the LORD."

The word "find" in the passage above is the Hebrew word *matsa*, which means "to find, meet, get." It refers to "finding someone or something that is lost or misplaced." It can also mean "to discover." And that tells us a bunch.

First, it tells us that we don't accidentally stumble into our mate. We must be intentionally looking to meet and to "match up" with one. That assumes that God is involved in the process so prayer and a sense of important attributes you would prefer to see in your spouse-to-be are part of the "finding, meeting, getting."

Except for pre-arranged marriages between families, this is exactly the process most successful bachelors use to become a husband. Most single men look for a certain type of women who fits their sense of preferences, dreams, belief system, personality and temperament, as well as other variables unique to the seeker's wish list.

Sitting at home hoping the phone will ring is not what God had in mind. Meandering through life hoping to get lucky isn't God's plan either. God wants his men to make a concerted effort to locate a mate, while submitting to the leading of God. It's a partnership deal. You are supposed to come up with a reasonable target – creating a list of preferable attributes AND to put yourself in the social environments conducive to finding that type of person. Then you should let God lead you through the active process of "faith" to intersect with a woman who's a God-given match for you.

Second, you are to be seeking a "wife" –one who corresponds to you. The word "corresponds," first used by God when describing the woman He will custom create for Adam, means one suitable to you – suitable spiritually, intellectually, emotionally, and physically. This woman should have a similar worldview, ambitions and interests – not your clone, but someone you feel close and comfortable with. Too many men have let media influence what they think is a match – some hot swimsuit model or nothing. Never mind that few are the models and fewer still the women who look good in a magazine without the touch-up measure of

Photoshop or an airbrush. No, we are to be looking for a realistic person who we can relate to in a balanced fashion, not just a sex symbol. (Read Genesis 2:18-25)

By the way, that brings up a caution. If you have a woman chasing you, there is a good chance she is not God's choice for you, unless you are a "blockhead" and can't see the "handwriting on the wall" about her. It is possible that God is resorting to having her help you wake up that your wife-to-be is standing right in front of you. Usually a woman seeking a man means more troubles later – trouble related to your love and affection for her, trouble about who will head the family as its loving leader, trouble about satisfaction, regret and commitment.

If you have a woman who is unashamedly trying to seduce you, run. Any woman that bold and shameless is not the quality of woman, typically, with whom you will want to build a spiritual heritage or family future. (Read Proverbs 9:13-18)

Finally, don't fret. Just let God guide you through the course of life. As you live your life, moving where God leads, you will often "accidentally" meet your potential spouse. Meeting the right one is hard to orchestrate, hence the flood of dating tools, online or otherwise such as e-harmony or Just Lunch, and the like. I think you should be open to everything as a possible path of God to your helpmate. You may bump into that person in a variety of ways: an online dating tool, a blind date, or your friend's girlfriends' friend. You may meet her at church, the gym, work or another social group.

You never know, but not looking while you're moving through life is a big mistake. Therefore, the more you want to find a wife, I believe you need to upgrade your efforts in two things: prayer and social involvement. Again, sitting on the couch Saturday night won't 'find you a wife," just a lonely night on the couch. (Read 1 Samuel 25)

Caveat for the married man: For those of you reading this who are married, I want to caution you from ignoring the notes above as "history" and therefore irrelevant for you. Instead, let me offer you two other thoughts.

First, if you are married I hope you see the genius of the pursuit and the satisfaction of accomplishing the "find" that God designed and sent you to fulfill. If so, stop and give him thanks before extending some appreciation to your spouse.

Second, if you mistakenly bypassed this godly ritual and found yourself married by some other manner than the biblical "seek and find" method, take courage. God tells us through His prophet Joel that He can restore "the years that the locust have eaten." In other words, God can bring blessing from what appears to be a problem. Ask him for that now, that your marriage will become, if it isn't already, all that he intended and designed, even though you sought an alternative to His divine plan for finding our mate. Give Him thanks and show appropriate appreciation to your spouse. (Read Joel 2:25)

Consider this: Read the following passages and ask yourself the questions provided

1. Proverbs 18:22 —How are you, by faith, actively seeking to find your wife?

2. Genesis 2:18-25 —What does your list contain for your "help-mate" — that is, the woman who "corresponds" to you? What do you have to offer (strengths)? What do you need from your partner (your weaknesses)?

3. Proverbs 9:13-18 — What does this passage say about the kind of woman that we should stay away from? And this passage, Proverbs 9:1-6 – what about the difference of this woman; what characteristics does she exhibit that we should look for in a wife?

4. 1 Samuel 25 — This narrative of David's conflict with Nabal also presents an interesting scenario of how God might introduce us to our wife-to-be. What was it about Abigail that not only attracted David to her but made her a worthy complement to the soon-to-be King of Israel and his professional, imperial role?

5. List some "best practices" for finding the wife of your dreams as you seek the best candidate, intentionally, courageously, honorably and prudently.

6. What about this statement: *"If a woman is pursuing you, I'd take some time to consider her motives. Best candidates are sought, not seductive."* Do you agree or not and why?

Prayer of the single man: Father in Heaven, I understand that getting married means I need to go find my wife; that is my responsibility. I also see that in your Sovereignty you assist by putting her in my path. So help me to walk in the right directions in life and be sensitive to your presence and attentive to the women I meet, that I might sense that she is the complement to me, my helpmate, who corresponds to me; my strengths supporting her weakness, hers, mine and yet both aligned on the most important issues of life – faith, hope and love in our Lord Jesus Christ. Amen

Prayer for the married man: Father in Heaven, I understand that getting married required that I find my wife; that was my responsibility. I also see better now that in your Sovereignty you guided me and assisted by putting her in my path. Thank you that through this process you enabled me to meet and marry my complement, my helpmate, the one who corresponds to me; my wife. What a joy to know that in your design I can offer strengths to support her in areas she is weaker, and she serves me similarly. Thank you that you craft our hearts to align on the most important issues of life: faith, hope and love in our Lord Jesus Christ. Amen

Value

Introduction:

Marriage is the topic of this brief study. So far we've seen that an active faith, one that looks for God's gift of a wife, ought to be part of the focus of a man's life who desires to marry. An active faith is the first of seven essential ingredients to becoming a good husband. We should want a healthy marriage and seek it diligently if we want to "find" the best woman God has for us. The next ingredient naturally follows: we will value our wife beyond all other human relationships.

Let's discuss that next.

Commentary:

#1 Value – Proverbs 18:22 — "He who finds a wife, finds a good thing and obtains favor from the Lord"

The phrase "good thing" is the Hebrew word *tob* – it means not only "good thing" but can also mean "benefit, welfare, beautiful, prosperity, enjoy and happy." How about that, men? Your wife is meant to add a beautiful, pleasant and prosperous aspect to your life. And, they really do, don't they!

How many of us are willing to admit they we wouldn't be nearly as well off today if she had not been a part of our lives?

Not only are the decorating and designer appointments of my home more beautiful and pleasant with her touch, but she is, personally, a beautiful and pleasing addition to my life. She adorns my life both at home and in social occasions. Plus, I have to admit that my whole life is more prosperous with her by my side, encouraging my efforts and adding a positive, motivating factor to my ambitions and work. Because of her, I want to enlarge my capacity for industry, saving, investing and expanding both my material as well as relational opportunities. I want a bigger and better life because of her and I want it for her. The truth is, my sincere desire is to serve her best interests, for two reasons. First, something inherent in me wants to be a blessing to her and give her my best. Second, I have learned from scripture, as well as from experience, that serving her best interests ultimately comes full circle to benefit me. (Read Ephesians 5:25-28)

I win twice because of her. I bless her and God blesses me. Truly, she is a good thing and I see the benefit to her as my partner in life. She is the right helpmate for me, making my life ultimately more beautiful, prosperous and happy.

Therefore my friends, I have to ask a question. Why is it we often resent the influence, advice and criticism she offers? In fact we've coined a phrase for her verbal challenges to our behavior and habits: we call it "nagging." We get so focused on defending our position against her "nagging" that an intractable conflict of differences begins to emerge. If we don't change our view and our response to her "criticism" we can harden into an angry, defensive marriage partner. Right?

I think part of the "nagging-conflict-disagreement-angry husband cycle" is developed because we've lost our view of our wife's value. When we begin to overlook the benefits she brings to the whole of our lives and overlook what motivates her "advice" or "criticism" (nagging) we devalue her personhood, lower the estimate of her worth and treat her as an adversary rather than the advisor and teammate that the "helpmate" role was designed to play.

In other words, although we may disagree with her opinion or how she states it, normally your wife is simply trying to help you, as head of the home, be a better blessing to the rest of the home – your domain. She is striving for excellence as a woman defines such things (read the definition of SARS in the book, *Man of Influence* by Jim Coté, Intervarsity Press). She cares about you, the kids, the larger family, your friends, your finances, property and future. When she "nags" you about your health, what you eat, what you drink or how you don't work out, she is saying, in words you can't hear, that she cares about your health and how your habits affect it.

Yeah, I know no wife is perfect and she has her own limitations, selfish desires and bad habits. But experience has taught me that most women are seeking the family's best interests when they suggest change, ask questions, or critique us. Therefore, we should value them at those times as well as when they are applauding our success. Either way — nagging or applauding — they are trying to drive us toward success.

Men, quit the whining and discipline yourself to achieve success. You can't afford to argue with a coach or boss who's critiquing you in an effort to point out ways you can improve. Neither should you dismiss your wife for doing so. Men, quit being so defensive about your wife's criticisms. Value her input, discuss with her your need for motivational balance and, if need be, your need for affirmation. And move on. It's unwise to fault our wife for telling us stuff no one else has the guts to mention. Use this input constructively and learn to see it as a useful tool for your growth.

Guys, you win when you show your wife how much you value her. God will reward you for leading and loving her. You lose when you don't show her because God is also capable of discipling you. God is apt to do so if you don't begin to show your wife that you value her. (Read 1 Peter 3:8, 9)

Caveat for the single man: Isn't it true that your search to find your wife begins with a value- oriented process. Typically guys look for value in the following normal terms: "She looks nice – pretty to me. She has a personality I appreciate and resonate with. Her values and views on life are similar and satisfying to me. She brings a quality of assets and life to mine that will enrich my existence." Right? Sure it is! Therefore, once you find her, don't ever quit looking at the positive attributes she holds for you. Those "attributes" will see you through tougher times of disagreement, dissatisfaction and conflict.

Both single men (looking for the perfect woman) and married men who've already found her, need to remember the following truth: There is no perfect partner, therefore, there is no perfect marriage. Neither one of you will be the perfect solution to all the needs and desires of the other. This is why an appreciation of value is so necessary. The more we reflect on the positive side of life and show gratitude for all the benefits we derive from our marriage, the more we will cherish our wife, pursue harmony, enjoy the moment and protect the covenant of our union with her.

Consider this: Read the following passages and ask yourself the questions provided

1. Proverbs 18:22 — List the things you value, the "good thing" you see in your wife. And you single guys, what is on your Top 10 list for the women you hope to marry? Write it out.

2. Luke 6:38 — Do you really believe that God will specifically reward you now for the things you do for others? Explain...

3. Do you realize that a redemptive marriage relationship is what we are called to provide to our spouse? Explain what you think of this definition of a redemptive relationship: "one that costs you something significant in order to unselfishly meet the needs of another whom you value." What is your view of that type of relationship? (Ephesians 5:25-28)

4. Ephesians 4:31, 32 — Explain how destructive words can make matters worse in a marriage argument and how, according to the above verse, we can overcome the tendency to hurt others with our words?

5. 1 Peter 3:8, 9 — The apostle Peter writes that we should be positive with others. He calls it 'blessing." The word blessing means "to speak well of." List legitimate compliments (well-spoken words) that you could give your wife to affirm her and bless her.

6. S.A.R.S. states a simple fact, men are most focused on four main
    motivational desires: Sex, Adventure, Respect and Success.
    Women have 4 different primary drivers: Security, Affection,
    Relationships and Stability. These differing drives in life typically
    cause most of the tension in a marriage and ultimately are the
    basis for every argument and the main driver for a wife's "nag-
    ging" the husband. How do you think that may be true, or not, in
    your marriage?

Prayer for both single and married men: Father in Heaven, I see
now that Scripture is clear, women are to be seen as a good thing,
to be cherished, appreciated, and valued. Therefore, I ask you to
help me see this value your way and remember it. Help me to live in
such a way that my wife sees, feels and knows how much I value her.
Indeed, that was my viewpoint from the beginning. Help me to never
lose this understanding and forgive me for the times I've forgotten
how much I need her. Also, Gracious God, help me to always to seek
the best for my wife, to treat her in a blessed way and to expect from
you that I will receive a blessing in return. Amen

Favor

Introduction:

Earning merit-based rewards is how the world operates. I remember the merit badges I tried to accumulate as a Boy Scout. Later in school, I learned that every grade was based on my effort, what I earned. High school and college sports were the same way: you made the team based on performance. You made the All-City Team based on excellent performance, or not! Business is that way too — you earn what you get.

Fortunately, this is not completely the case in marriage. Certainly, you will get out of marriage what you put into it. Bless your wife and you will receive blessing, but demean, ignore or marginalize her and you will get nothing but trouble. There is more to marriage than just what you deserve. The Lord Himself gives a miraculous blessing. He gives it simply because you stepped out by faith, to care for one of His daughters, through your marriage commitment. That blessing is called favor from The Lord.

It is to that miraculous blessing, promised by God, that we now turn our attention.

Commentary:

#3 Favor – Proverbs 18:22 — "He who finds a wife, finds a good thing and obtains favor from the Lord"

Men, God will bless you through your wife, just because He promised to. Your part in enjoying that favor is to believe it, expect it, acknowledge it and give God the credit for it; thanks! You also need to show your wife favor. That is the gift of what she needs from you – loving leadership and appreciation.

"Favor" in the verse above is the Hebrew word "*ratson.*" It means "goodwill, favor, acceptance, pleasing, delight, desired." It is akin to the New Testament word "*charis*" from which we get the word "grace, unmerited favor." This means that we get from God, what we don't deserve. We receive His unmerited favor, God's best for us, when we actually deserve the worst.

The core concept of the Gospel explains that Jesus died for us, taking the punishment of our sin-debt and paying the price of that sin (which we deserved to pay), death. See the following verses for further study: Genesis 2:16-17; Ezekiel 18:4; Romans 3:23 and 6:23. Grace is the word scripture uses to describe what Christ Jesus did for us as redemption – meaning He paid the price to buy the debt of the debtor so the debtor goes free. We don't deserve pardon, but punishment. Yet pardon is what God gave, "unmerited favor"!

The Apostle Paul states it this way in his letter to a church in an area of Asia Minor called Ephesus: "for by GRACE are you saved, through faith and not of yourself, it is the GIFT of God; not as a result of works, so that no man may boast" (Ephesians 2:8,9).

How does this divine blessing relate to marriage? Perhaps an example from a story in my life will make it clear.

A few weeks ago I booked the travel, lodging and transportation for my wife and me to celebrate our anniversary. This trip to the West Coast would begin in Sonoma, California, and end in Orange County a few days later. The trip involved two separate airline tickets for two one-way trips: one ticket to get there for each of us and the same type of tickets for our return from two different airports. It also involved hotel stays in four different cities. Plus, we needed a one-way car rental from Sacramento, California (our destination city), to Orange County (our departure city).

As you can see, it was fairly complex, but hey, this is what I do. I travel a lot and am a pro at booking trips. Except on this trip I screwed up!

When we got close to our first hotel stay, I discovered I had mistakenly booked a hotel in Sonora, California, about 5 hours away from our intended destination. Since I had an appointment for us in Sonoma the following morning, we could not use the Sonora hotel.

I told my wife the mistake and we prayed about it in the car. I prayed God would help me get another hotel in Sonoma, even though a NASCAR event there made that prospect improbable. Nevertheless I got on my iPhone to find a hotel. Several calls later I only confirmed my worst fears – every room was booked.

I persevered in calling and it finally paid off. I found a decent hotel with one room – a nonsmoking King – in a nearby town. It was too good to be true but I asked the lady to reserve it for us. Then I asked for the price. Ouch, it was WAY more than our budget allowed. So I asked for any discounts – AAA or AARP? Alas, there were no discounts since the event traffic canceled any discounts. So I nicely asked the reservation host if there was ANY other way she could accommodate us at a lesser price. She told me to wait and 10 to 15 minutes later, my patience running thin, she came on the phone with good news. She found a way to give us that room for $99!

Wow, we took it. I thanked her profusely and hung up. Excitedly, I told my wife the good news on the room price to which she calmly announced that she had been praying "God would favor me and give me a really good deal."

Wow, again! Though I didn't deserve this goodwill, I received it as a gift from God who answered the prayer of my wife.

That is just one simple example of how God has shown me gifts beyond my merit, simply because He chooses to confirm His promise to bless me on behalf of my wife.

As I look over the landscape of my life, since being married I found countless other examples of blessings I've received from being married to my wife — blessings "exceedingly, abundantly beyond all I could think or ask" (Ephesians 3:20). There have been countless surprises, good things, produced in my life through my wife. The honest truth is, I would not be here today if it weren't for her. My life would not have the rich satisfaction I currently enjoy, if I had remained unmarried.

Make sense? Then let's discover how this can work in your life too.

Consider this: Read the following passages and ask yourself the questions provided

1. Proverbs 18:22 — What do you think of this concept of favor? Do you believe in it or think it unimaginable that you can get from God things you haven't worked for or don't deserve?

2. Proverbs 18:22 — If you agree with the biblical truth of "favor," then list the "goodwill," the good things, you have received that directly relate to your wife — her influence, her industry, her faith, her strengths and gifts. Write it out.

3. Ephesians 2:8, 9 — What do you think of Jesus's redemption of you? What do you think of this verse, about the unmerited favor of God available for you, in Christ, through faith? Explain...

4. Now, since you are receiving blessings you do not deserve, simply because God is blessing you on behalf of your wife, list ways in which you could return the "favor" to her. How can you bless her – in word, deed or otherwise?

5. What about this, men. Wouldn't one small way you could thank God and show appreciation to your wife be to always speak well of her, to others, when she is not with you? Too many men think it's cool to belittle the "missus" when she's not around. Don't you think it rude and unfair to say unkind things about your wife to the boys you hang out with? Make a list of ways you intend to speak and do well to your better half.

6. Psalm 106:4 — "Remember me, O Lord, in Thy favor toward thy people; Visit me with Thy salvation" This verse in Psalm 106 is a prayer for God's favor, generally, and his overall deliverance, specifically. How might this verse show us both the desire of God's goodness toward his people, as expressed by the psalmist, as well as the need for His people to specifically seek His goodness, his favor? Would that not also include the "favor" of God through marriage?

Prayer for married men: Father in Heaven, I repent of the unkind, rude and disparaging remarks I have made to my wife. I really never realized that you are looking at me more favorably because of her. God, because You choose to bless married men, I now commit to looking for specific ways that you are doing so. I commit to changing my view of my own "merit." That is, I realize that my strength, savvy and successful performance isn't the sole reason for my success. Your favor is the reason and your favor is displayed in my life because of my wife. Help me now, to do a better job of showing her my appreciation. Please forgive me for any and all disparaging words I have ever spoken against her. Help me now to live gratefully, expectantly before you and appreciatively with her. Amen

Prayer for single men: Father in Heaven, I do want your favor in my life. I want your salvation from sin; I want your overall deliverance from all evil. I also want to receive positive benefits of your goodness, your favor toward your people. Since you are a God who distributes favor and since you specifically distribute this favor to men who have found a wife, I pray for a wife suitable for me and the favor that shall result from the commitment to one woman in marriage. Amen

Conflict

Introduction:

Take any marriage enrichment class or read any marriage book and you will find that the two most often addressed subjects are first, communication and second, conflict. Typically the first leads to the second; a lack of communication or poor communication skills inevitably lead to conflict.

But that is not all. Conflict can emanate from many sources. Each of us is imperfect, sinful, selfish and have a host of inner and outer motivational factors that can result in having conflict with our partner. Some people even seem to have the gift of conflict; they know how to start a fight and let it linger!

What does conflict create? If it isn't recognized, sorted out, repented of and left behind, inevitable division enters the relationship that can ultimately lead to dissatisfaction, separation, and even divorce.

That is why this subject is so important to understand, so necessary to confront and so essential to manage in the marriage relationship.

However, to truly understand marriage conflict we have to look at the beginning of marriage and see the biblical basis of this issue.

Commentary:

#4 Conflict – Genesis 3:16b — "... In pain you will bring forth children; Yet your desire will be for your husband, And he will rule over you."

The first conflict recorded in scripture was between God and His adversary (see Genesis 1:2). God resolved that conflict through creation. The second conflict is recorded in the third chapter of the same book with man rebelling against his creator, God, and His ordered law. This led to God's judgment and one aspect of that judgment was an inevitable and interminable tug of war between man and his wife. They began a control battle about who would lead the relationship as head of the home (see Genesis 3:1-19). A host of negative outcomes resulted from that one sin that haunted both the man and his wife for the duration of their lives and were passed on to their progeny.

The main focus for this article is the revelation of an embedded conflict that God pronounced, as a consequence of their rebellion in the garden, would now, ever after, be a part of marriage.

Sin always brings negative consequences and conflict between humans is one proof that the created order has been upset through our sin. It is a maxim that one reaps what he sows. No one ever sowed corn and reaped gold coins. Similarly, no one ever sowed rebellion and harvested true peace.

This biblical, historical event undergirds the causal basis for conflict within marriage. In Genesis 2:15-17, God declared an inviolable law – "don't eat the fruit of that one tree; if you do, you will die" — but the married couple ignored Him, ate from it and immediately suffered the death of innocence, intimacy and harmony. Now, through inherited sin, we all suffer the result of their rebellion — lifelong rebellion in our hearts, the lifelong search for harmony in marriage, the ever-present seed bed of conflict.

How can this be? This is how. This is the biblical theology of conflict: In the beginning (Genesis 1:1) God created "order" out of chaos. Genesis 1:2 describes the chaos, and Genesis 1:3-31 displays God's resolution; a progressive order is created. The capstone of that order was the creation of man – literally mankind (Genesis 1:26-28). God then gave them dominion over all of creation. This word "dominion" (Hebrew: radah), literally means to rule with "a strong sense of authority, without compromise." Furthermore, He gave the male headship over the woman in their co-regency (see Genesis 18-23; 1 Corinthians 11:1-3; 1 Timothy 2:12-14) and assigned him the accountable privilege of ruling over the home as "head' of his wife.

This headship is to be exercised with respect and a sense of spiritual equality (Genesis 3:16b; 1 Peter 3:1-7). However, when God assigned man to "rule" the woman, He pronounced a different type of rule. God used the Hebrew word *mashal,* which speaks of a "rule" that has more of a peer aspect than the word *radah. Radah* connotes more of a sense of dominance than *mashal. "Mashal"* means "to lead in a fashion that respects the other's dignity and assignment as an under-lieutenant." With dignity, recognizing the difference in design, role and responsibility of each spouse, the husband is to rule his wife, literally, "as a Governor over a lesser Governor."

Unfortunately, the reason God set up the marriage relationship this way is a result of man and woman's failure to obey His ultimate rule over them, as evidenced by their disobeying Him in the garden. As a result, God judged them both in the area of their primary responsibilities — man in his career, as he was assigned, to provide and protect; and the woman in her role in the home, supporting her husband as helpmate and bringing forth new life in the bearing of children.

To ensure that there was a clear understanding of the God-given chain of command, God established a hierarchy. In Genesis 3:16 He announced His punishment for the woman, *"to the woman He says, I will greatly multiply your pain in childbirth, in pain you shall bring forth children; yet your desire shall be for your husband, and he shall rule over you."*

With that, the marriage wars began. The woman has been seeking to control the man and his "rule" in the home since millennium past. And that same conflict is present today.

There is much more to the story and to the dynamics of this intrinsic marital conflict, such as man's refusal to communicate, to stand up for God's prohibition when the woman sought the forbidden fruit, as well as his lethargy in leading, leaving her unprotected from the serpent, and letting her do the dirty work of "providing" food without a word of caution (Genesis 3:1-6). The judgment stands and for good reason. Men and women struggle in deciding who's to lead, who's responsible for family decisions and who's ultimately in charge.

Oh, and one more thing. The judgment spoken in Genesis 3:16 is NOT just about sexual desire and childbearing. Nope, it is about the dynamic setting in the home, about headship and hierarchy – man, woman, children. The passage is saying that despite her natural disinclination to breed, due to the pain of childbearing, women will still pursue procreation but the male will still be in charge. By divine fiat the woman is consigned now to be the helpmate she was created to be, though her "desire" will be to usurp his headship platform. Nonetheless, her God-given charge is to help her husband lead the home and raise the children.

Today we get that confused. Too many men won't lead so their wives must. Or they marry a strong, talented women and so capitulate their accountability before God to answer for the health and welfare of the home because they don't have the courage to face the conflict. Instead, they once again leave it to the wife to "do all the dirty work." Another option is for the married couple to get it wrong and let the kids dictate how the home is to operate. So you end up having juveniles leading adults. Who's leading who in that scenario?

Both ways are wrong biblically, but they are sadly manifest in many couples' lives today. The role reversals are a blatant continuation of our rebellion against God's spoken word and it is the reason so many marriages are in trouble today. If you want to get it right, if you want God to bless your marriage and childrearing efforts, then do it His way; do it biblically.

Men, you need to step up, take responsibility. You need to communicate. You need to care for and protect your wife. You need to provide her a safe and successful place to help you raise your children.

You say you can't see that happening, given your circumstances? Then repent of your lack of faith. Take God at His word and step out in His confidence to work, pay the bills, get a safe home for the family and trust God to provide you with everything He asked you to do as you lead and serve your family.

Trust me. You do it His way and you will find even the most hardheaded woman amenable to your Christ-like leadership, sooner or later. Trust me, I've seen it happen many times. Okay, don't trust me. Trust God!

Consider this: read the following passages and ask yourself the questions provided

1. Genesis 1:2 — Notice the four factors of chaos presented here. They are all manifestations of Satan's impact on an environment. Tell me how you now feel about the necessity of God's order in your life.

2. Genesis 1:3-31 — Notice the progressive nature of God's creative order. This is still the way He works as He brings order out of chaos. This is why it takes a while to see His changes in a life or a marriage. How does this fact affect how you will now step forward to work on positive change in your life and marriage?

3. Genesis 2 — Read this account of God's creation. Notice it gives more detail than the outline presented in chapter 1. What do you glean from this passage as it relates to the value of your wife or His intent for marriage? How does it humble you?

4. Genesis 3 — Read this account of the rebellion of man and woman against God. Do you see the parallel of their sin and His punishment? What about God's solution – to cover their sin exposure by taking the life of another? – of one of the creatures Adam just named in the garden (Genesis 2:19,20; 3:21)? Do you see the beginning of the sacrificial system God instituted with Moses (which culminated in Christ, the substitutionary Atonement, substituting one life for another)? (John 1:29)?

5. What do you really think of male headship in the home? It flies in the face of the modern feminist movement so how do you feel? How does your girlfriend or wife feel about men leading? What does the word of God say to you (Genesis 18-23; 1 Corinthians 11:1-3; 1 Timothy 2:12-14)?

Prayer for married men: Father in Heaven, wow, I see now that conflict is inevitable because we are all sinners and rebellion is in our nature. I see now that the only way to minimize conflict is to seek to live all of life your way – whether culture approves or not. I now see the need to diagnose our competing points of view early, to discuss them, to acknowledge when we sin, and to repent and apologize for how we hurt each other. I know, Lord, we will never get this perfect, but help us to do this better so we can enjoy the peace and harmony you originally desired for married couples to enjoy. Amen

Prayer for single men: Father in Heaven, wow, I see now that conflict is inevitable because we are all sinners and rebellious in nature. I see now that the only way to minimize conflict in a relationship is to seek to live all of life your way – whether culture approves or not. I now see the need to work on this now with the women I date. I also see it would be a benefit to discuss this issue with any prospective wife to see how she views the home, leadership and responsibilities in the home and other factors of male and female roles. I know, Lord, I will never get this perfect, but help me to do this better and find a wife who shares my point of view so we can enjoy the peace and harmony you originally desired for married couples to enjoy. Amen

Sacrifice

Introduction:
Last week we looked at the privileged leadership position that men hold in a marriage relationship, as ordained by the Lord: "head of the home." That "headship" is much debated and much disputed by the modern viewpoint of gender equality. No doubt much of the debate stems from the failure of men to provide the kind of leadership ("headship") that God intended. Men seem to come in two flavors: dominating dictator or absent abdicator. Men can sin on either extreme of their call to headship. One extreme is lording dominance over the wife. The other is to mercilessly leave her to do the job of guiding and guarding the relationship while you remain MIA in the marriage.

If the world at large only knew what men are called to be and to do in this headship role, they would welcome it for it has nothing to do with dominating or abdicating and everything to do with sacrificial service in love. The role men are designed to play in marriage is to replicate Christ to their wife. As Jesus gave up His glory (Philippians 2:5-8) and the rights and privileges of his Divine prerogative, so too are men to give up in marriage. Christian men are to consider their high position in marriage as a call to humble, redemptive service. We are to give of ourselves, dismissing our right to certain prerogatives, in order to seek the highest good of our wives – even if (and especially if) it costs us greatly to do so.

To this most difficult concept we now turn our attention.

Commentary:
#5 Sacrifice – Ephesians 5:25 — "Husbands, love your wives, just as Christ also loved the church and gave Himself up for her…"
The verse above says it all and in just 17 words! Just as Christ gave up His life to redeem all mankind, men are to be ready and willing to give up whatever is necessary to serve the best interests of their wife, especially when she has need of his strength to supplement and support her own.

This is really the definition of *agape* love, the word most used to speak of Christ's love for us as well as the motivating factor of His redemptive sacrifice for our sins on the cross. We needed someone holy to pay for our sin. Jesus was the only sinless person alive. He lovingly *(agape)* gave up his life in order to buy back (redeem) ours. This is the gospel, the best example of love, and this is what men are asked to provide their spouse in marriage. We are to ask this question, "What does she need that she can't deliver on her own?" We need to make decisions based on the following consideration, if you have the capacity and ability, will you do it? That is the question to answer — a question of offering Christ-like love.

It is redemptive to give something precious of yourself away when necessary to bring another person out of pain, perplexity or a problem to safer, securer ground in life. How loving, how redemptive, when a husband gives of himself in precious, sacrificial acts to help his wife become the woman God wants her to be. Redemptive leadership supports her effort to fulfill God's calling as a wife, mother and minster of Christ's love, as a "fellow heir of the grace of life" in conjunction with her husband.

What does that kind of sacrifice look like, this redemptive leadership? It looks like giving up 5 hours on a golf course on Saturday during the season of life when your wife needs you at home to help her with the children and to help in the home with tasks such as shopping and cleaning. It demonstrates your humility and wisdom as you "get" the big picture of family life, helping her to help you as she strives to bring order out of the common chaos of family life.

It looks like a management function, men. It is tantamount to a cash flow issue. In this case however, the cash flow involves your time, abilities, money, goals, dreams, and recreation. It may even challenge your career designs. You have to learn to budget your life in order to serve the higher interests of a godly family, making sure your wife is well resourced to handle her part of that effort.

We live in an era when it's a challenge to budget life. This is the era of two-career couples, extended families living far from each other, attention distracting media, super mobility and conflicting child activities, all of which want to be at the top of the priority pyramid. This mix of overlapping family obligations creates prioritization divisions between many spouses. As head of the home, men, you will be forced to make selfless and wise decisions as to what wins first place, second, third and so on. You will have to ferret out these priorities with your wife – the needs over the wants, hers and yours.

As a result, you may find that loving your wife as Christ loves the church may mean that you do not spend your vacation whitewater rafting in the mountains but driving your family to your in-laws so your wife can see her parents and they see your kids.

It may look like buying a minivan instead of a pickup. It may look like getting a four-bedroom house instead of a new ski boat. It will no doubt look like helping the kids with homework and cleaning the kitchen so your wife can go to the gym or to an evening Bible study for women.

Redemptive leadership also knows when to say no. It is Christ-like to say a necessary '"no" when it best serves the greater goals and good of the family. This too is an essential characteristic of your headship, men; a perspective that is the husband's responsibility to know and to guard. Admittedly, this is particularly challenging if you happen to be married to a strong-willed woman but courageous love and leadership steps up to do the right thing despite the potential fallout.

Redemptive leadership often looks like saying "no" to her when saying "yes" would be an easy cop-out, so as to prevent an argument and necessitate an explanation. Redemptive leadership occasionally needs to say "no" to her going shopping with her friends when you know the budget has just enough money for a new set of brakes for the car and not a new pair of shoes. Or it can look like saying "no" to her when she wants to have a lady's night out but this week you need the kids sequestered so you can study for your exam on a post-graduate program you're trying to finish.

Redemptive leadership and the dicey decision making that goes along with it looks like having the Wisdom of Solomon, which God will give you if you ask (James 1:5). This wisdom knows when to say yes to serve the better interests of your wife, when to give up something you want in order to give her what she needs. Finally, it knows when it's best to say "no" to her – even if it causes a conflict.

Jesus said, "Greater love has no man than this, that one lay down his life for his friends" (John 15:13). Since our wife is our best friend, it is loving and redemptive to "lay" something down to serve her needs. Sometimes the "laying down" is a giving up of a personal want. Sometimes that "laying down" is to say "yes" when you'd rather say "no". Sometimes laying down your life for her means saying no and suffering the disagreement that comes with it. That is leadership. That is doing the dirty work. That is strength of conviction. That is courageous love in a relationship most meaningful to you. That is being the man of God you are called to be in a marriage – Christ-like.

Consider this: read the following passages and ask yourself the questions provided

1. Ephesians 5:25 — This passage presents the concept of sacrificial love in a marriage. Does this shake up your view of a husband's leadership responsibility and style in marriage? How so?

2. Ephesians 5:25 — This verse essentially presents the concept that marital love, from the husband's vantage point, is spelled "sacrifice." It is Christ-like love, *agape*, seeking the best for the object of your love. List a few sacrifices that you need to make right now in order to best serve your wife redemptively.

3. Ephesians 5:26-27 — According to this passage, the return on the investment for *agape* love is a reward that makes it all worthwhile – you get her back "sanctified" (in a better position than before). For giving up something special to you, something sacrificial, you get back a "best wife"! Tell me how that changes your view and motivation for the sacrificial path of loving your wife as Christ loves you.

4. James 1:5,6 — Do you sense you could really use God's wisdom to know best when to say "yes" to her and when it is best to say "no"? What is the issue, are you afraid to transgress her turf? Do you think she will get angry or something? What is it that makes this a challenge?

5. John 15:13 — Is your wife your best friend or not? Should she be or do you wish she were if she is not already? Either way, how can you best show her your friendship, your *agape* love today?

Prayer for married men: Father in Heaven, what a concept this is; the love of Christ in my marriage, exercised by me?! I am not sure I can do this. I admit today that for starters I am selfish and when I get a chance, I want to do and to keep what is most important to me. Yet today, I am beginning to see that your way and her best interests are really more important than the optional things I want. The challenge is that my wife is selfish too. I don't think it's right or fair to give up my stuff if it is only going to reinforce her selfishness. So give me your wisdom to know when to do what. Also, I hate conflict. I pray for the courage to stand up and do what is right even though it may provoke the ire of my wife. Give me the strength to do the right thing, to stand my ground and wait for you to work on her to learn to submit to my leadership when I am doing what you want me to do, that we both may grow in our relationship with you and in harmony with each other. Amen

Prayer for single men: Father in Heaven, what a concept this is; the love of Christ in marriage, exercised by the husband?! I am not sure I could ever do that. I admit today that for starters I am selfish and I really never considered that I would have to give up myself and my stuff to serve a wife's best interests. I am going to have to grow more mature in Christ to even be willing to do this. But I do want to get married and I am reading this material in order to prepare myself for marriage. Give me the capacity to change from a selfish guy to a Christ-like servant/lover of my wife. Heavenly Father, bring me a woman who has the capacity to live with me as I learn this redemptive leadership style that we both may grow in our relationship with you and in harmony with each other after we wed. Amen

Understanding

Introduction:
One of the big issues in marriage is our knowledge of our spouse. Wise husbands become students of their wives. That may seem weird or boring or unnecessary, but if you are like most men you are constantly trying to figure out how women think. Am I right?

If not, then you may be the kind of guy who hasn't really thought about it. Or maybe you just don't care. Maybe you intend to simply pursue marriage your way and hope it works out. Or perhaps you are shallow enough to believe it isn't a matter of intelligence and skill, it's a matter of your overwhelming charisma and charm which your wife can't resist and therefore will follow your thoughtlessness about her? Maybe you've just never thought about the "homework" part of getting your marriage successfully to its grand conclusion, "until death do you part"?

Some men think marriage is simply a matter of the percentages or luck. Somehow you roll the matrimonial commitment dice and see if you get snake eyes or not? Or perhaps you think that relationship knowledge is important, but for you it's a one-way street, your way or the highway. She needs to study you and do things your way, always. Some men honestly believe they're the only one that matters and it's up to the wife to figure them out and "get on board." The divorce rolls are full of guys like that. Are you one?

No matter what you think about studying your spouse, I know three things that are true about the benefit of being a student of your wife and

I want to share them with you. One is that God cares and He has written to us about this necessary tool to use for a "best practices" marriage. Second, your wife cares that you get to know her. Third, you should care because you will be the benefactor of a better marriage, a happier life, and the blessing of God. Let's look at this subject right now.

Commentary:
#6 Understanding – 1 Peter 3:7 — *"You husbands in the same way, live with your wives in an understanding way, as with a weaker vessel, since she is a woman; and show her honor as a fellow heir of the grace of life, so that your prayers will not be hindered."*

"Understanding," now that's tough. The English definition is as follows: "A mental process of a person who comprehends; *superior power of discernment; enlightened intelligence, knowledge of or familiarity with a particular thing; skill in dealing with or handling something."* Are you kidding, "understanding, intellectually" is a major component of marriage? Is that what I am about to broach with you guys? Yep.

Am I saying that we married guys need to become some sort of marriage "professor" to have a good marriage? Sort of.

Does the Bible have something to say on this issue of marital knowledge? Yep, and the verse only adds to the importance of this issue. The passage we'll be looking at today is from the Apostle Peter's first book. The passage is found in 1 Peter 3:7. The word used in that passage is the Greek word *gnosis*. It's a word that literally means to "know, have knowledge of, to come to know." It assumes a growth in knowledge of a particular subject. Even to "have faith in." Gee whiz, that can be a tall order!

I have trouble understanding others, even greater trouble believing them or believing in their perspective. Heck, I have trouble understanding myself, much less someone else. Although I am a relatively optimistic and self-confident person, I must admit that the longer I live the more I have self-doubt and "relationship doubt" when I think about what I really know about others or believe to be in them. Can you relate?

How do we move toward a proper understanding of our wives and do so in such a way that it adds to a healthy confidence in them, greater appreciation and more harmony in our home?

It's as easy as one, two, three. First, care enough about her as a person that you want to get to know her better. That is really called love.

Second, be willing to accept that what you find is her intrinsic self, and don't focus on changing it. Focus on enjoying it, that is, enjoy what you learn about her. Roll with it, enjoy her and figure out ways to enhance her positive traits. For example, if she is studious, don't knock on her when she wants to read a book and not watch the NBA Finals with you. Or if she's aggressive, be careful not to over-challenge her and send her off a cliff of irrational action.

If she likes nice things but you all can't afford them, help her to draft a personal budget and lead her in living within that cash flow framework. Or if she is stronger at things than you are, like family financial management, by all means let her manage the checkbook and family finances. You just need to stay tuned and review it regularly with her so that you, as the leader, know what's up. You cannot abdicate leadership on anything that is part of your headship responsibility in your marriage and family finances are one of them. When you pass off to your wife one of your management responsibilities, remember that you are ultimately accountable to God for the outcomes and one day you will have an "eternal life review" with Him about it. Let her be the manager when she is more capable than you but stay connected to the operations as the head of the home.

How do you find out what her relative strengths and weaknesses, likes and preferences, are or aren't? By being a marriage professor, by being a student of your wife. Does this make sense?

Third, don't stop learning and leading. This will be a lifelong workshop, men, and there are two reasons you will be studying your wife for a lifetime. One is that God made her complex and He made her different than you. To better understand this subject I recommend that you read the fine book, *Recovering Biblical Manhood and Womanhood*, by Wayne Grudem and John Piper. This excellent work details some of the differences between men and women: biological, psychological and sociological. As a result, you will see not only the differences between you and your wife but some of the complexities of the female mind, body and emotions. And that leads to an interesting second reason to study your wife.

The second reason you need to study your wife for a lifetime is that she will change. Oh sure, her basic temperament and giftedness will remain but as she matures and as her body ages she will likely change some of her preferences, viewpoints, feeling and the way she processes things emotionally, intellectually and physically. This labor of love, being a student of your wife, is the gift that keeps on giving!

Don't be alarmed at that. If marital blessing is the outcome of your homework, this is a sure path to lifelong blessings. God will bless you through your wife, as we stated in the third study, both because she is there and because your "studies" honor the Creator who made her for you!

Furthermore men, we need to understand that studies alone will not make your marriage better – only academic. You must apply what you learn if you want this to work well and not just become an intellectual exercise in futility. What you learn about your wife, what you begin to comprehend about her (as complex as it may be), you now need to apply to benefit her in *agape* love.

Indeed, that is exactly what the word "way" is meant to convey in the phrase "understanding way."

The definition means "manner, mode or fashion." It has to do with the character or habitual manner of the understanding. It means you should move from knowledge to action as it also means the "method, plan or means for attaining a goal."

In other words, "way" means you will find a way to apply what you learn about your wife so that you two reach the goal of harmony, blessing, mutual satisfaction and the fulfillment of the covenant you made before man and God, "until death do us part."

Finally, here is a note from scripture on how we as Christian husbands need to treat our wives.

The last half of the verse from 1 Peter 3:7 ends with a one-two punch on risk and reward. We have a commandment to grant her honor as a fellow Christian (see Galatians 3:28,29) followed by a warning "that your prayers may not be hindered." This brings perfect balance to the relationship in a Christian marriage – there is room neither for spiritual sloth nor chauvinism on the part of the husband. Do this, men, respect your wife's spirituality and support it. Do not lean on her in spiritual dependence rather than lead as you were created. Get this wrong and you risk unanswered prayer. Get this right and you reap the reward of a better and more effective prayer life.

Consider this: read the following passages and ask yourself the questions provided

1. 1 Peter 3:7 — Tell me, is all this marriage student stuff driving you crazy or driving you to be a better husband by going to school on your wife, and why? What are some of the things you have already learned about your wife? Which of these most surprised you after you were married?

2. 1 Peter 3:7 — What do you think of the warning about risk and reward in this passage? Which of the two improper extremes do you tend toward: spiritual sloth or chauvinism? And your wife, do you have to encourage her to develop her faith in the Lord Jesus or is it her, pressing you? Do you two pray together? Is there anything holding you back from praying with her?

3. Are there some things in her life that you feel she needs to unlearn, things that are simply entrenched conditioning and not a part of her intrinsic temperament and personality? Are there legitimate things that she needs to work on so that your marriage will be better? You know this is also a way to apply what you learn of her – constructive criticism. Of these things how will you lovingly help her to move on and be a better wife? And, likewise, what are some areas you need to move on from as well?

4. I recommend Piper and Grudem's book. It will illuminate the second part of 1 Peter 3:7 as well, for it will explain what "weaker vessel" means, giving you greater empathy for your wife, as she tries to keep up with you physically. It will also explain why she focuses on relationships more than you. It will, furthermore, help you answer critics by crafting your own viewpoint on how men and women are similar and how they are different, although equal politically, spiritually and humanly. Will you get a copy and read it?

5. 1 Timothy 2:8-16 addresses male headship in the home and church. It was written by The Apostle Paul under the inspiration of the Holy Spirit. What does it tell you of your spiritual responsibilities before your wife?

Prayer for married men: Father in Heaven, I never dreamed marriage could be so much work. First I have to go to school and then I need to implement what I learn. It all makes perfect sense but frankly, I am tired at night and just want to coast at home. I see I can't do that. I am on the job at home too. Give me the desire, stamina and focus I need to work on my marriage by studying my wife and then applying my "findings" to our relationship so we can better enjoy your blessings. Amen

Prayer for single men: Father in Heaven, I never dreamed marriage could be so much work. If married men are expected to go to school on their spouse and put that "learning" into action, perhaps I need to be a better student of the women I date and get into this habit now. It just makes sense that it would give me a leg up and help me be better prepared for marriage. Help me to pay more attention to the women I date in order to see what I can learn that will make me, ultimately, a better husband when I "find" the one you have provided to me as my helpmate. Amen

Respect

Introduction:
Respect, ha! Men demand it, will fight over it, and often don't deserve it. But it's a God-given marriage ingredient nonetheless.

Think about it men, when you boil your conflicts down to the core issue, most of them involve a lack of respect. When you feel slighted by someone else your sense of self-respect and self-worth click in, prompting you to stick up for yourself, right?

It is that way at work, sports, and in neighborhood relations. In all of your relationships with others, especially men, you are wired to want respect. Respect (or the lack thereof) is why you get upset when another motorist cuts you off on the freeway, or a fellow employee cuts you off mid-sentence in a business meeting. It is the basis of most fistfights and lawsuits. It is the core issue that creates the impulse that made you mad and willing to fight or sue your opponent.

Respect in life is normally based on merit. We say a person does or does not deserve respect. But marital respect has a component to it that is not merit based. It is simply commanded, expected and the wife has the task of providing it. What's difficult about this concept as it relates to marriage is that a man's level of worthy behavior isn't a prerequisite for his deserving respect.

Respect is simply to be delivered by the wife, by faith, just as men are to deliver *agape* love to the wife, by faith. In acting out of faith in the goodness of God and in obedience to His commands, they are both trusting God to make something special out of their effort to trust and obey Him. No matter the deservedness of the spouse they seek to love or respect, they are believing God for His promise of blessing, harmony, peace and longevity.

Respect from the wife to her husband is based fundamentally and spiritually on the husband's created and given position in the home. It is similar to the military code of saluting, or respecting rank even when a person's character may be less than desirable. Rank matters in the military and position matters similarly in marriage. The wife has the assignment of honoring the husband's position, his hierarchal responsibility, which he must bear as he leads and loves his wife.

To that proposition we now turn our attention.

Commentary:
#7 Respect – Ephesians 5:33 — "Nevertheless, each individual among you also is to love his own wife even as himself, and the wife must *see to it* that she respects her husband."

The word used for respect in this passage is really the word "fear." Literally, this New Testament Greek word, *"phobeo"*, means "to put to flight, to terrify, frighten, fear, awe, respect." What does this type of fear or respect mean? How is it to be applied? Those are two important questions we must answer.

For starters, don't let the lexical meaning, as strong as some of those words are, fool you into thinking you are now a superhero worthy of worship and meant to strike fear into the heart of your beloved wife. No, no, no. Instead, see that definition as a cluster of words that help provide proper meaning for a misunderstood concept such as respect and do so in a proper context. Given that we are talking about marriage and not an imminent invasion from your worst enemy, we know that our wives are not to fear us like Attila the Hun or Ivan the Terrible. Instead, we are to adopt the plain vanilla meaning of respect and see it as a synonym for awe.

The wife is to be awed not by your greatness as a superhero but by your standing before God as the one who is accountable on behalf of the family. Since God ordained and called man to lead woman, her utter respect and reverence for God ought to be translated in some measure to you in acknowledgment; i.e. respect!

I repeat, the basis for this hierarchal arrangement is not to demean a gender but by Divine design. The Bible simply showcases the Architects' design for marriage as man standing between his wife and God in spiritual accountability. Husband, you stand before God on behalf of her in responsibility, to lead and steward the gifts God's given you, including your spouse and children. That is a heavy responsibility, fraught with challenges but no matter, it is what God ordained and that ought to be the end of the debate.

The wife should be in "awe" of God who chose man for this role and reflect some of that awe to her husband who must bear it. That need not be viewed as a disrespectful, belittling, or diminishing thing but simply a fact of divine design, that husbands serve God in serving his wife's needs.

This meaning of this word helps us to arrive at a proper interpretation of the text. Context is helpful in understanding the word of God when culture or unfamiliarity bleed into our viewpoint. Context helps us get a fix on the word "respect" when we look at the word "subject" in verses 21 and 24, as well as the proper interpretation of verses 22, 23. Those hotly debated verses suggest two things. First, each Christian is to respect the role and rank of others and yield to their specialty, their authority, when that authority is known. In other words, we are to respect the roles, jobs, assignments, gifts and station of others and not seek to usurp or demean their role.

The second application of this hierarchal verbiage is reaffirmed in the marriage context (verses 22-24) and gives us a clearer picture of the marriage arrangement with respect to authority, or who's leading whom in the home. The text clearly indicates that the man is to lead and the word used in this passage is a Greek military word, *hupotasso*, which means "to rank under." That squares perfectly with the intent and need for respect in verse 33, where the wife is told to respect her husband. Furthermore, the parallel passage in Colossians 3:18 supports that definition. It is a theological fact that man has the higher "rank" in the marriage union! As I've said before, it's because the husband has been assigned this rank by God and he will give an account to God, alone.

Please remember, preconceived notions of how we think things ought to be, especially when living in a pluralistic culture ignorant of God's word and intentions will inevitably lead us into misunderstanding the real meaning of God's word. When you add to the fact that we live in a world pushing an androgynous oriented, gender neutral, sociological ideology, truth about marriage relations can easily be clouded by popular opinion. It is essential to do our homework when it comes to Bible study. We must ferret out God's meaning when we do. Word studies can help us do that. Looking at the broader context can help us do that. Cross-referencing with other similar passages can help us come to a right understanding of what God said and what He meant.

We must remember that God wrote to tell us the truth about marriage relations, way before this generation decided to change the gender paradigm on leadership in marriage. Biblical doctrine is not democratic. We really don't get a vote on who is the head of the home. Nor do we vote on whether a husband must love his wife as Christ loved the church, or whether the wife must respect her husband as he bears more accountability than she.

Consider this too, the book you read, when you read the Bible, is one written by men inspired by God with the truth. For example, the book of Ephesians was penned by an Apostle — someone handpicked by Jesus Christ to explain His viewpoint to the world and to announce the theological basis of marriage and family. Because of this we should respect the Bible as a holy book, divinely inspired by God. Men, listen to God first, not culture.

All of this helps to explain the meaning of the verses quoted from Ephesians 5:22-33.

Men, you can expect pushback on this one. No one will hammer you for showering more *agape* love on your wife but boy, oh, boy, watch out when you tell her she's supposed to give you respect and "rank under"' your authority in the home, whether she wants to or not! There are at least four reasons why it will be difficult to get her on board with this.

1. She is human and we are all rebellious against authority.

2. It galls the modern woman to think any man has authority over her. Her whole educational life she has been told by family, teachers, media types, celebrities and the federal government that she is not your subordinate but your equal. She has probably even been told recently that she is your superior!

3. You may not deserve respect.

4. She may not know what the Bible teaches or care!

So what are you to do? First, you are to love her unconditionally. You are to act with decorum worthy of respect. You need to pray with her. You need to look at scripture together. You need to teach her what God has said, making sure that you are applying it to your life as well!

You must give her space and time to come around to God's way of thinking. Believe me, God has ways to get your wife to do what He wants her to do as it relates to you, especially when He sees you are trying to follow Him with all your heart. You can count on the work of the Holy Spirit to change your hearts, your way of thinking, your behavior and lifestyle patterns as you pray together, interact with scripture, worship together and seek God's will in your marriage life.

God's plan for marriage is not complicated. It is just that people don't really know His plan because they have never taken time to look into it, to study it. You just did, in this seven-week course on marriage. Congratulations! You already have a leg up on most couples.

The second problem with people not functioning in God's plan for marriage is that they are resistant to a biblical life style, preferring the world's. I hope that is not you.

If you are truly a Christian man you trust Christ as your Savior — God's only Son who gave up His perfect life to pay the penalty of your sins, who rose three days later from the dead, proof that He was God and your sins are forgiven. If that defines your faith, then you have what it takes to have a great marriage, a biblical marriage.

To that end I pray for you.

Consider this: read the following passages and ask yourself the questions provided

1. Ephesians 5:33 — This verse is clear, your wife is to respect you. In what ways does she or does she not do this now?

2. Do you operate in a way that provokes her respect or her ire? Biblically you are to receive her respect for the institution of headship whether you exercise respectable behavior or not. But how can you be a better husband and so live up to the respect you are to receive?

3. Ephesians 5:21 — "Be subject to one another in the fear of Christ" In what ways do you two show a healthy mutual respect to each other? In what tangible ways do you yield to her greater strengths in your marriage as a way to affirm her personhood and contribution to your marriage?

4. Ephesians 5:22, 23; Colossians 3:18 — What does, or will, your wife think of this concept, of her submitting to your higher "rank" in your marriage? If you expect pushback or mockery, will you bring it up or ignore it? What does that say of your leadership, your faith, your love of her, your self- respect?

5. Write a one sentence description of a biblical marriage from the noble vantage point of two, mature, self-respecting, secure Christian people. Should this sentence be your motto for your marriage?

Prayer for married men: Father in Heaven, marriage is complicated when viewed from today's standard perspective. But marriage is a beautiful balance of love and truth, respect and courage, when viewed through the lens of scripture and your design. Thank you for these seven reminders of what a biblical marriage is meant to be and how it is to work. Help me and my wife to move more fully in the direction of your lordship as well as your design for marriage, so that we may achieve a better balance, stronger harmony and fuller measure of your blessing in our union. In Jesus' name, Amen

Prayer for single men: Father in Heaven, marriage is complicated when viewed from today's standard perspective. But marriage is a beautiful balance of love and truth, respect and courage, when viewed through the lens of scripture and your design. Thank you for these seven reminders of what a biblical marriage is meant to be and how it is to work. Help me to use this biblical perspective as my base line for developing my marriage when I "find" a wife. Help her and me to move fully in the direction of your lordship as well as your design for marriage so that we may achieve a better balance, stronger harmony and fuller measure of your blessing in our union. In Jesus' name, Amen

Notes

Notes

Notes

www.ingramcontent.com/pod-product-compliance
Lightning Source LLC
Chambersburg PA
CBHW071438040426
42445CB00012BA/1391

* 9 7 8 0 6 1 5 9 6 3 3 3 4 *